Poems, Essays And Comments FOR Everyone

Ian Mayo-Smith

Kumarian Press

Cover design by Beth Gorman
Copyedited and proofread by Linda Lotz
Designed and typeset by Jenna Dixon

Printed in the United States of America on acid-free paper by
Bookcrafters. Text printed with soy-based ink.

Library of Congress Cataloging-in-Publication Data

Mayo-Smith, I.
    Poems, essays and comments for everyone / Ian
    Mayo-Smith.
        p.   cm.
    ISBN 1-56549-043-6 (alk. paper)
    I. Title.
PR6063.A934P64   1995
821'.914—dc20   94-39164

98 97 96 95 94   1 2 3 4 5
1st printing 1994

Contents

Foreword

Ian Mayo-Smith has lived an interesting life. His travels have taken him to fifty-three countries and he has lived and worked in Europe, Africa, and Asia as well as the United States.

His talents, interests, and enthusiasms are many and varied. His career started in intelligence work and progressed to administration, teaching, and international consulting. He has written books and articles on public management and training. His photographs have appeared in national newspapers in England, Nigeria, and Tanzania as well as in photographic magazines and other publications. Although he disclaims any skills as a performer on any musical instrument, songs he has written have been performed in a number of countries. He also has an ability to make us laugh. He considers one of the highlights of his career to be writing the words and music for a theatrical revue in Tanzania (which he also produced and acted in), which brought together people of all races for the first time in what had previously been a predominantly white amateur dramatic society.

But of all Ian's talents, it is his ability to reach and touch people through his poetry that we celebrate in this book, which is timed for publication on his seventieth birthday. Although individual poems of his have been published in various publications from time to time, this is the first time his poetry has been published in collected form.

I have no illusions about this man. After all, I have been married to him for nearly twenty-two years. Initially, when I first met him and we had to work together in Kenya, I found him difficult to work with. In fact, I complained to our joint boss about him. But in the end, who could resist a man who used to place on my desk, before I got to the office, his latest piece of verse, especially as it would often be a love poem! But after we were engaged to be married, my mother told me, "I know why you are going to marry this Englishman of yours. It is because he makes you laugh!" Well, after twenty-two years, he still does, and he still writes poetry.

I hope you will enjoy it too.

Krishna Sondhi
Kumarian Press

Acknowledgments and Dedication

First of all, this book owes its existence to Krishna, who has been the inspiration for much of the poetry I have written, and who has been a constant source of encouragement.

Secondly, there are others who have helped bring some of these poems to life. In some cases I have dedicated specific poems to them. But there are others to whom I have not dedicated specific poems, and I would like to acknowledge them here. In particular I would like to mention all those who took part in the evening of "Poetry, Entertainment And Comedy for Everyone (PEACE)" in the Caux Cafe this past August when the New Beatniks (Sam Pono, Ed Howard, and I) tried to recreate the atmosphere of creativity of the Beat generation. Sarah Smith arranged the evening and sang for us. Sam and Ed provided the music. Marie Goodman Hunter gave a memorable reading of some of the poems. Heide Goertzen sang and read, and Mary Lean and Melanie Trimble read other poems from this collection, helping to make it a truly memorable evening.

Thirdly, in order to produce this book in time for my seventieth birthday, the whole production had to be done in record time. I owe a large debt of gratitude to Jenna Dixon who designed and typeset the book, to Linda Lotz who copyedited the manuscript, and to Beth Gorman who designed the cover.

This book is for all of you with my thanks.

Ian Mayo-Smith
West Hartford
September 1994

Poems,
Essays
And
Comments
FOR
Everyone

Some of the poems in this book were written in Switzerland at Mountain House, Caux-sur-Montreux, a beautiful place halfway up a mountain and overlooking Lake Geneva. Mountain House is an international conference center known throughout the world for its work in creating an atmosphere of peace and compassion in which reconciliation, personal change, and conflict resolution become not merely possible but imperative.

High up in the mountains
I look out over the lake
Where a mist forms,
So I cannot see clearly
Into the far distance.
Yet even so, I can see much farther
Than ever I could
When down on the ground.

(Caux, July 1994)

Experiencing the pain of the world
I find freedom.
Acknowledging the hurts I have caused
I find liberation.
Accepting the hurts I have felt
I burst my chains.
Wanting nothing,
Expecting nothing,
I have enough and to spare,
A surplus to give away.

(Caux, July 1994)

This is a dance with subtle movements.
This is music with a subtle beat,
Sung in a language with unfamiliar inflections.
This is a dance for dexterous feet.

Watch the feet of the dancer moving.
Watch the expressions on the dancer's face.
Watch the dancer's hands and fingers
As the dancer moves with exquisite grace.

The Lord of the Dance beckons us forward,
Beckons us to put our feet to the floor.
The Mother of the Dance sings so sweetly
That we could go on dancing for evermore.

So follow her steps in the early morning.
Keep on dancing throughout the day.
Follow wherever his flute shall lead us.
The dancers lead us on our one true way.

(For Vijayalakshmi Subramaniam;
Caux, August 10, 1994)

If I hurt you
Or stand idly by
While others do,
It is I and my children
Will suffer
When the wheel comes around
As it will.

If I blame you,
Say it's all your fault
That I'm suffering now,
It is I and my children
Will languish
In a desert of pain
And despair.

If I care for you
And we heal our hurts
And the others too,
It is we and our children
Can flourish
When the wheel comes around
Once again.

The idea for the next poem came from Leonard Johnson, a young Londoner of Jamaican descent whose own personal change and dedicated hard work have brought new hope to the community where he lives in Brent. At a meeting at a conference on "Hope in the Cities," Leonard commented on people's skepticism about the possibility of a change in human nature. "People say a leopard cannot change his spots, but we are people and we can change," maintained Leonard, speaking from his own dramatic personal experience. So this one is for Leonard.

The leopard cannot change his spots.
Whyever should he care to?
He obeys the laws of leopard life,
The life that he is heir to.

I can't change the color of my skin,
Which makes me different from others,
But I can change the attitude within—
See all mankind as sisters, brothers.

The leopard kills and eats his prey
In the way that leopards should do,
But I can live another way
As all us humans could do.

The leopard obeys the laws assigned
By God for leopard life,
But, forgetting what God told mankind,
We find we're locked in strife.

Thank God I'm not a leopard
Destined to kill and destroy.
I know it's right for leopards
Though they don't seem to get much joy!

I've never seen a leopard
With a smile lit up by love,
Poor chap he has no shepherd
To guide him from above.

But we were made to listen
And we were made to care.
God's law for us is different,
So we had better hear.

We'd better hear and act upon
The law that's made quite clear;
To live the way we're meant to,
With love and without fear.

No grasping, no addictions
To food, drugs, money, sex;
No gossiping, no lying.
It's simple not complex.

And if we fail to do so
We'll live as leopards do,
And if you don't kill me, you see,
Watch out, or I'll kill you.

(Caux, July 20, 1994)

If you've ever tried to meditate, I am sure you have come across the problem described in the next poem.

Oh, mind of mine
If you don't mind
I'll ask you to be quiet.
I always find
My restless mind
Behaving like a riot.
It's very bold
And uncontrolled,
Moves under its own power.
Oh, how I itch
To find a switch
To still it for an hour.

I wonder why
That though I try
To make it rest a bit,
It sees no cause
For it to pause
And ceases not a whit.
"Don't hesitate
To meditate"
I tell myself each morn.
My only aim
My mind to tame.
It seems a hope forlorn.

In the fall of 1992, Krishna and I visited South Africa. It was the first visit for her, though I had previously been in South Africa for overnight stays on my way to Botswana and Lesotho. We had never been there together, since we are a mixed-race couple. We saw many encouraging signs in that country and encountered much kindness from people of all races. I wrote the following poem in the lobby of the hotel where we stayed in Braamfontein, Johannesburg. I dedicate this poem to my good friend and fellow Beatnik Sam Pono.

Waiting in the hotel lobby
I sit seeking inspiration,
Watching the scene
Unfolding before me—
The black porters and security guards;
The receptionists, black man, white woman.
The young white man
Playing pleasing music
On the piano.
The hotel guests
Are all colors
Of the human rainbow.
They speak Japanese, German,
French, English, Afrikaans,
And African languages I cannot recognize.
There are plenty of smiles
And people act kindly,
Politely to one another
In this quiet haven in this city
Where crime is so common
And people live in fear
Of theft, muggings, rape, and murder.

Birth is a painful process
And what I am seeing

Is the birth of a new nation;
A phoenix rising from the ashes
Of an outdated society
That never could have grown
Into an adult member
Of the world community of nations.
But this new emerging order
Has such potential,
Faces so many dangers,
Has such needs
For understanding
And for leadership
That we can only pray
That God will bless it.

(Braamfontein, October 1992)

This next poem is for Marie Goodman Hunter, who read this and other poems in this volume so beautifully one evening at the Caux Cafe.

It's incredibly beautiful
To sit and watch a sunset
At the end of a day.
You can see sunsets only
When the sky is clear—
Not too many clouds about.

It's incredibly beautiful
To look at a friendship
That's grown throughout the years.
You can see a friendship only
When the sky is clear—
Plenty of love about.

It's incredibly beautiful
To see the dawn come up
At the beginning of the day.
You can see the sunrise only
When the sky is clear—
Not too many clouds about.

It's incredibly beautiful
To watch young children growing
At the beginning of their lives.
You can see them growing only
When the sky is clear—
Plenty of love about.

I love to be beside the sea
And watch the sunset.

I love to sit with friends
That I've known long.
I love to see the sunrise
On a fine spring morning.
I love to see the hope
And love in children's faces.

But even if I can't have this
It's still incredibly beautiful.

(December 15, 1993)

Radiant, like a sunburst,
Your face looks out to me
From the photo in my album.
Warming my spirit,
As the sun warms my body,
The smile in your eyes,
Even when I see you
Only in my mind's eye.
Your image brightens my day.
May God help me
To brighten yours.

(Caux, August 1994)

As a Buddhist, I try to follow the Noble Eightfold Path laid down by the Lord Shakyamuni Buddha for his followers. This is never easy, and for me one of the most difficult aspects of the path is Right Speech. This means never saying anything that is untrue or unhelpful and—this is the most difficult part—never gossiping about others behind their backs!

It isn't malicious gossip.
It's only a friendly chat.
We talk about this and the other
And then about this and that.

In the course of our conversation
We may mention a name or two
But that's only to be expected
And it's just between me and you.

I can't be blamed if I mention
What John was doing last week.
I think you should know about it.
It would be wrong of me not to speak.

And as for what Mary was up to!
Well, I can't keep quiet about that.
She said such bad things about you.
She's really a spiteful cat.

I hate all these scandalmongers.
They do so much harm, you see.
I just wish they would learn to keep quiet
And refrain from gossip like me.

As a grandfather with nine grandchildren, I often feel appalled at the state of the world that they are inheriting from people of my generation. As a Westerner living a comfortable life in the United States, I am painfully aware of what my generation has failed to do to improve the lot of the billions living in Third World countries, including those parts of the Third World that exist in North America and Europe, particularly in our inner cities.

My brothers, my sisters,
I weep for you.
I cannot enjoy the comforts of my life
When I see how you live.
I cannot feel much concern for the state of my bank
    balance
When I see your poverty.
I cannot complain at unfair treatment I've received
When I see you so exploited and victimized.

You were not born
In some comfortable home in the West
As I was.
Nor did you have some powerful protector
Who lied and cheated and stole
And thus became respectable.

How can I reach out to you?
How accept you
As having equal rights with me,
Equal claims upon the earth's bounty,
That earth which we have savaged?

What can I do to bring about
That state which

In our hearts
We reach out for
But hardly expect to see?
Where justice is for all
And everybody's needs are met
In a healed and healing world.

Maybe the answer to the questions raised in the poem above can be found in the one that follows.

Brick by brick
The house is built,
Yard by yard the road
And the harvest
Of renaissance
Seed by seed is sowed.

Piece by piece
The jigsaw, this divided world,
We repair
As one by one
New friends we make
And barriers down we tear.

So hour by hour
Just stay attuned
And listen to your heart
As step by step
You make your way.
Each day is a new start.

(June 14, 1994)

Buddhism also teaches the dangers of grasping and delusion and ways to overcome these two evils. The next poem describes a lady who learned the hard way.

Mary, Mary, quite contrary
Found herself an adversary,
Married him and later, of course,
Sued the fellow for divorce.
Took him for everything she could.
It didn't leave her feeling good,
But she felt it necessary
Because he was her adversary.

Mary, Mary found employment.
Got satisfaction, if not enjoyment.
Climbed the ladder, you can guess,
Always looking for success.
Mary made a lot of friends
Of those who could help her attain her ends
But discarded as refuse
Those who were to her no use.

Mary nearly reached the top,
But then her advancement seemed to stop.
The top positions were all filled.
"They'll have to go," our Mary willed.
"For me to rise, they have to fall.
I'll have to fix them. That is all."
So Mary schemed, manipulated
Till they were all eliminated.

Mary, Mary, quite contrary
Saw everyone as an adversary.
If not right now, then maybe later,

So she became the eliminator.
Mary, Mary smoked a lot.
Mary drank gallons of coffee hot,
Developed ulcers and a bad heart too.
Oh, Mary, what have you done to you!

Mary still had one more fight.
She knew that something wasn't right,
But what to do? And where to go?
This time Mary didn't know.
Her therapist, her doctor too
Told Mary just what she must do.
"Slow down, Mary, before it's too late.
Why don't you learn to meditate?"

Now Mary, Mary, quite contrary
Has found a brand new adversary,
The toughest one she's ever fought,
More slippery than Mary thought,
For it's her very self she's taming—
At least that's where our Mary's aiming.
And she understands that that'll
Be an uphill, long-term battle.

But Mary's less contrary now,
Pleasanter to be with anyhow.
She's made up with some of her old foes.
At least that's how the rumor goes.
Her health is better than before.
She laughs and smiles a whole lot more.
She still has a long way to go
But she may get there yet, you know.

(July 7, 1993)

*Even when we think we are enlightened and unselfish,
we need to be careful to take a closer look at our motives.*

I only want to serve.
When I play tennis
I only want to serve
An ace straight down the center line,
Leaving my opponent standing.

I only want to serve
In some honorific capacity,
Perhaps as chair of some
Important task force or committee.
It's not the image or the status.
I only want to serve.

I only want to serve
The people of some
More disadvantaged country,
Humbly passing on the expertise
That I've acquired
And which they desperately need.
I only want to serve.

I only want to serve
And I resent the fact
They do not always
Follow my advice
Or that they criticize
The fees I get
And the special privileges
I enjoy,
For I only want to serve.

But sometimes late at night
A nagging question
Buzzes in my ears
Like a persistent bee.
It quite unfairly asks me
Who is it after all
That I only want to serve.

True friendship may be the greatest gift that we can either give or receive. The following poems are about friendship.

Who knows if he really is a friend?
Who knows if she really at the end
Will stand by me,
While others curse me and revile me?

Who knows what he says behind my back
Who smiles at me when I'm with him face to face?
Who knows what she will do when I'm under attack,
And maybe in disgrace?

I promise you my friend that I will not betray you
By agreeing with those who say you
Have been at fault and wrong.
That will not be any part of my song.

But I may openly and in private challenge you
If ever I believe you are not true
Unto yourself. And I ask of you
That you will do the same for me.

I do not want to talk of blame.
To my mind we are all the same,
All fallible, sometimes strong and sometimes weak
And so of shame and guilt we will not speak.

But we will try
To hold our vision of each other high.
That's what I'll do
To show my love for you.

(April 26, 1994)

The eyes of love see clearly
All my ugliness and imperfection
But see beyond them
To the shining diamond of my heart.

The voice of love speaks clearly,
Very down to earth and real,
Setting up a resonance,
Striking answering chords within my soul.

The ears of love hear clearly
All the trivialities and gossip
With which my talk is filled
But listens for the wisdom words
     that come from deep within.

The heart of love beats strongly,
Never faltering, eternal,
Beats in time and beats in tune
With all the other hearts throughout the world.

The mind of love knows clearly
Without sentiment or bias
With a wisdom that goes far beyond
The wisdom of the world.

The hands of love reach out
To touch, to hold, to steady me.
If I become love's servant
Then shall I be truly free.

Intimacy

I want no barriers, no fences
Twixt you and me,
No evasions, no pretenses.
I want to tell it like it seems to me
And hear you telling what you see,
Turning no blind eye.
Let's be like that, you and I.

Synergy

We two can do
A better job
Than twice either one.
It's also much more fun.

If I had to name two specific aspects of the evils of grasping, fear, and delusion that continue to cause the greatest problems of our times, both nationally and internationally, I would have to name racism and religious intolerance.

I have a vested and personal interest in combating religious intolerance, for I was brought up as an Anglican Christian and became a Buddhist. My wife's father was a Sikh and her mother was a Hindu. One of her brothers is married to a Muslim. One of my sons, together with his family, is a dedicated evangelical Protestant Christian. Another is married to a Jew, and I have three grandchildren being brought up in the Jewish faith. My youngest son, whose wife is Spanish, became a Roman Catholic. So within my own family almost all the major faiths of the world are represented, yet we are united in our fundamental beliefs.

I tried to summarize my feelings about religious tolerance in the following poem.

My friend Jesus talks with me.
My friend Buddha walks with me.
I can live my whole life through
Walking and talking with these two.

My friend Krishna laughing comes,
Playing his flute and humming his hums,
And sometimes he teases me
As I spend time with these three.

Now here comes the Prophet, look,
With wisdom from the Holy Book.
He adds his voice to our discourse,
Compassionately speaks with force.

Other voices too I hear
From a distance in my ear.

To different accents they are leaning
But all convey the selfsame meaning.

Slow down. Be quiet. Listen. Be still.
Be free from the fetters of self-will.
Put others first and then rejoice,
Obeying the insistent inner voice.

According to traditional Buddhist belief, we have all been reincarnated thousands and thousands of times, so that at one time or another in previous lives, we have been each other's mother, father, child, brother, sister, aunt, uncle, spouse, or grandparent. That being the case, it is absurd for any one of us to hurt another, for in doing so we may be hurting our past or future mother, child, wife, and so on. One doesn't have to believe in Buddhism to benefit from the concept of universal relatedness.

Sometimes in the morning
As I sit and meditate,
Eyes closed,
I see your face
Before me,
You, my friend.

My breath goes out.
My breath comes in.
My consciousness
Is fixed upon it.
But through this consciousness
Your face appears, your image.

I recognize that we're not separate,
You, my brother, you, my sister,
My son, my daughter,
Mother, father, spouse,
Uncle, cousin, aunt,
And we have always been
Strands in the same weave;
Waves in the same ocean.

So how can I look on you
With anger?
How with jealousy, resentment,

Anything but love?
How can I want anything
From you,
Save that you be you?

For we are never separate,
But all are one
As all the waves
In all the oceans
Are not separate
And cannot be pulled apart.

To say that you can be less than me,
That I can be less than you
Is madness.
To think that I can gain
If I can make you lose
Is lunacy.
For if you lose, I lose,
And if you grow, I grow.

So let us choose
To recognize
No one is separate.
Stop hurting our left hand
To benefit the right.
My friend, within our hearts
We've known this
All along.

Sometimes I wonder what would happen if the Lord Buddha or Jesus Christ or the Holy Prophet were to return to earth today. What sort of welcome would they get—even from those who call themselves their followers?

The Buddha came back
So we killed him.
All his dangerous talk,
Taking the Eightfold Path
Quite literally.
I mean take his ideas
About right livelihood,
Not earning your living
At the expense of life.
So what's to become
Of the farmers who grow tobacco,
The men and women
Who process it
Or who sell cigarettes?
What's to become of them?
And what about all the millions
Who deal in arms or use them
In their daily work,
The people at Sikorsky,
Pratt and Whitney,
Electric Boat, to name a few,
And the army, navy, air force,
Marines, even the police who try to keep order
In our crowded cities?
What would we do without them?
No, these crazy ideas
Of an idealistic visionary
Are too dangerous, not just impractical,
So we had to get rid of him.
His other ideas were just as bad.
Right speech. What nonsense!

What would happen if we only spoke the truth?
Newspapers, advertising,
Even our daily conversation
With our neighbors.
All would have to go.
More jobs would be lost,
And many of us would have to stay silent,
Not saying a word.

I'm sorry, Lord Buddha,
Maybe you were all right
In your day.
Maybe what you said
Was suited to those simpler times,
But this is now.

And so you had to go.
It was not difficult
To raise up public opinion against you.
You and your dangerous talk.
You should have known
From your brother Jesus
What happens to those
Who want to upset the applecart
And shine the brilliant light of truth
On all our dirt.

And yet the trouble is
There will still be some
Who take you at your word
And who will shape their lives
According to your teaching,
Hard though it may be.
It would be ironic, wouldn't it,
If, though we have tried to kill you dead,
We find you triumph in the end?

Along similar lines, one Christmas I had these thoughts.

Why did he come,
Suffering the discomforts
And indignities of birth,
His least dignified of all,
In a farm outbuilding?

Why did he come,
Seeking the friendship of men,
Quarrelsome, untrustworthy, and self-seeking,
And of women,
Bitchy, vain, and possessive?

Why did he come,
Defenseless and knowing
We would wound and hurt him,
Let him down,
Condemn and kill him?

Did he not feel the pain?
Did he ignore the cruelty
And the weakness in us?
Could he not see we'd fail him,
Not once but again and again?

Strange that he took the trouble,
Strange that he saw us as his friends, his family,
Saw all the weakness and the evil in us,
But called us to be his equals,
Sons and daughters of God.

Common to virtually all religions is the idea of the law of Karma—that you reap what you sow. It may seem a harsh law, but did you ever think about what would happen if the law were repealed?

What a twentieth-century drama,
They've repealed the law of Karma.
You can act without thought, in a hurry;
There's not the least reason to worry
About the consequences of your acts.
There'll be no retribution.
What a wonderful solution.

But I'm afraid, without doubt,
It just isn't working out,
For though I no longer face
Any punishment, disgrace,
Or other penalty for what I've done,
I'm not having any fun.
For I'm the victim now, you see,
Of what the others do to me
And I can't make them desist
Since Karma does not now exist.

It's not at all what we foresaw.
Let us reinstate the law
And we'll just accept the fact,
Be responsible for every act
We take and accept the consequence.
Unfortunately nothing else makes sense.

As already referred to previously, one of the greatest problems of our age stems from racism and all other forms of discrimination based on differences in skin color, gender, religious or cultural orientation, and so on. I had always considered myself to be rather free from such prejudices, but when I took a really deep look inside, I found that this was not the case. In fact, I began to see that very few, if any, of us are totally free from such prejudices. However, we can learn to recognize the prejudices in us and to let go of them. Through the help of friends of other races and religions, I have been able to develop a little insight, as expressed in the following pages.

Confessions of an Ethnocentric Sexist Racist Snob

"I am not a crook," declared Richard Nixon, and entirely believed what he had said. "I am not a racist," said I, and my wife shook her head and smiled. "Look at my record," I said. Had I not, when a young junior member of the senior civil service in Nigeria, invited my Nigerian colleague to dinner? I shared an office with him and he seemed a nice chap, so it had seemed natural to invite him to our home. Only later did I learn that I was setting a precedent. It was not done for British expatriates to invite their Nigerian counterparts to their homes. My superiors looked at me askance.

And wasn't it true that later in Tanzania, when I found myself elected vice chairman of the Arusha Arts Society, the local music and dramatic society, I managed to transform that society from one that catered only to the expatriate and, to a lesser extent, the Indian communities to one in which people of all races got together and put on cultural events for the benefit of the whole community? I still have among my treasured possessions the earthenware jar signed by all the members of the cast and crew of the revue that an Indian colleague and I produced. Most of the signatures have faded, but there were African names, West Indian names, Indian names, English and American names.

And more recently still, was it not true that while I was working at the University of Connecticut's Institute of Public Service, where for six years I was director, our house in West Hartford entertained guests from all over the world, from Papua New Guinea to Pakistan, from Ghana to Guyana, from Botswana to Bhutan?

As for sexism, isn't it true that during the time I was director of the institute I got more women appointed or promoted to senior positions than had ever happened before or since? And even now, am I not content to be vice president of the company that we jointly own, while my wife is president?

So how can I be called a racist or sexist?

When I look back on my early childhood and school days, I was taught to believe that Great Britain was the greatest country in the world. It was not an exaggeration to say that Great Britain was divinely entrusted with governing at least a quarter of the globe. It also followed that all right-thinking people were members of the Episcopal Anglican Church. Jews seemed to me like aliens from another planet who somehow lived among us, and you could not really trust them. Roman Catholics were often nice and good people who for some strange reason went to different places of worship, where they burned some smelly stuff called incense and practiced strange rituals. I did not really have any opinions about Asians and Africans because I did not know any people of Asian or African descent. Such people just did not live in our neighborhood. But it was implicitly understood that they were inferior races and it was the job of white people, like my family, to govern, civilize, and educate them to our way of thinking and our way of life.

I remember when I was in kindergarten being invited to the birthday party of a little Jewish boy, Michael Jacobs. I went in some trepidation, for I knew that Jews were not like "us." And it turned out I was right. Michael's family was different. He seemed to have a lot of aunts, and they all seemed to show their affection for Michael in a very vocal way that just would not have happened in my family.

As for sexism, I was taught that the man was the head of the house. He should be the main breadwinner. I remember the contempt my father had for an uncle, actually the husband of my mother's older sister, whose income was less than that of his wife, my aunt. This contempt was not much softened by the fact that Uncle Ted had one paralyzed arm but was never heard to complain or demand any special treatment because of his disability and played very good tennis and golf. I also remember the severe rebuke I got from my father when as a recently married man I turned to my wife and asked her opinion before answering some question from my father. He turned to me and said, "Haven't you got a mind of your own? Why the blazes do you have to ask your wife before you answer my question?"

With this kind of upbringing, I feel that I can honestly claim to have come a long way. Many things have happened to make me question the original assumptions I learned at an early age. Perhaps more than anything else that has changed my attitude has been the friendship I have received from people of so many different racial, ethnic, and religious backgrounds around the world: my Muslim friends in Nigeria, Pakistan, and Brunei, for example; my Communist Party member friends in Vietnam; my many Hindu and Sikh friends in East Africa. The serenity of some of my Thai Buddhist friends impressed me so much that I came to study Buddhism and now call myself a Buddhist. Perhaps the good Lord wanted to teach me and my family a special lesson in tolerance. Otherwise, why would he have made me fall in love with and marry an Indian woman in Kenya whose father was a Sikh, whose mother was a Hindu, and whose sister-in-law is Muslim? And besides that, he has given me three daughters-in-law: one dedicated English evangelical Christian, one Spanish Catholic, and one Jew. So I now have three Protestant, three Catholic, and three Jewish grandchildren.

As for sexism, I can only say that it would be extremely difficult for anyone who was married to my wife to hold to views of male superiority. Her mother was a remarkable woman who broke many precedents in her own community in Mombasa, Kenya, where she became deputy mayor. She had a slightly forbidding exterior that hid a sense of humor and a sense of responsibility and caring for others that I have never seen bettered. My wife is very much her mother's daughter.

It would be very easy for me to say that I have overcome ethnocentricity, racism, religious intolerance, and sexism; to claim that I am cured of these related diseases. Unfortunately, the truth is that, as with alcoholism, it is never safe to say that you are cured. All these forms of prejudice are insidious, and sometimes they affect us without our realizing it. For me, this creeps in most often when I fail to listen carefully when people of different backgrounds express views that differ from mine or when I fail to have the same high expectations of people of another group as I do of people of my own group. It is something that I still need to watch all the time. Also, I have to realize that when I think that I really understand a person with a totally different background from mine, I am usually wrong. I cannot fully understand because I have not shared that person's experience. What I can do is to respect that other person and his or her views. And I can empathize with that person. Only then can I work with that person as a brother or sister.

So I confess to being an ethnocentric sexist racist who often falls into the temptation of feeling superior, but I can only plead that I recognize my problem and say, like a recovering alcoholic in Alcoholics Anonymous, that I am a recovering racist and a recovering sexist.

An unusual and inspiring conference took place in Richmond, Virginia, in June 1993. It was called "Healing the Heart of America" and subtitled "An honest conversation on race, reconciliation, and responsibility." As part of the conference activities, a Unity Walk through Richmond was organized in which various scenes from Richmond's history were reenacted. There was great emphasis on the role Richmond had played in slavery and racism, and it brought into my heart many things that I had known only in my head. It was a very moving experience. For the first time I began to understand what people like me had done to people who, like many of my friends, had black skins.

Since that time, through the friendship of certain people, notably Audrey Burton of Richmond, Rev. Mary Moore of Philadelphia, and Margy Palmer of Chicago, I was able to begin to try to see things from the perspective of an African brought to the United States as a slave and as an African American of today.

The poem that follows is dedicated to them.

My soul is bruised
For I am not a person. I'm a chattel.
These cruel people
With sharp noses,
Cold blue eyes,
Straight hair and pale skin,
So strange and ugly looking,
Took us in chains
And brought us to this land
In filthy, stinking ships.
Many died amid the stench
And sickness of that voyage.
We who survived
Were kept in prison
To be sold as cattle.
They beat us with whips.
They tortured and raped us;
They hanged and burnt us.

And worst of all they spoke
Of a god of love,
A god of compassion.
Sent to save our souls.
They, who had no love
And no compassion for us,
They told us of this God,
This Christ who came to save us,
And then they would not let us
Worship Him.
They told each other
All men were created equal
But as slaves we were not equal
So we could not be human
But something less.
And so we suffered
And we hid our anger
But it grew.

And now today
The laws have changed
And we are free
And those pale people
Think that all is well.
They do not see
That they will have to pay
For what they did
And what, in different ways,
They do today.
They do not see
That they cannot avoid
The Karma they've created.
They cannot see
Their world is gone
And never can be brought back.

And even now
Most of them cannot see
That there is still a choice
They have to make.
There is and will be blood
And death and cruelty.
It's too late to escape that fate.
But we can still avoid the worst.
We can avoid the holocaust.
They can choose to weep with us
Over the shameful past,
Or they can choose
To weep over the graves
Of sons and daughters
As we have done and do.
But they must face the truth,
Own up to it;
See what it has done to them;
And what it has done to us;
And come to us in humility
As full brothers and full sisters
Serving that god of love,
God of compassion.
Then they will find more and more
Dark answering hands
Outstretched to grasp
Their pale hands.
And we will break down all barriers
Until we realize the dream
That not only were we
Created equal
But our lives are based
On that equality
And that compassion
And that love.

Apart from the inherent wrongness of racism, it is at least partially the cause of many of the other ills that plague so many of the world's major cities. It is certainly a factor in the serious situation that exists in Greater Hartford, where I live. The following poem about the city of Hartford is based on recent events.

Things are moving in the city of Hartford,
Moving with the speed of bullets
Leaving children dead on the sidewalk.
Things are moving fast.

Things are moving in the city of Hartford.
State troopers are moving in
To help the city police deal with the gangs.
The gangs are really moving, man.

Things are moving in the city of Hartford,
Moving so fast that even as we mourn a child's death
Gunfire breaks out outside the funeral home.
That's how things are moving.

Things are moving in the city of Hartford,
Moving me and moving others.
Oh, my sisters, oh, my brothers
What have we done? What can we do?

Things are moving in the city of Hartford,
Moving just a few to seek the causes
Of this anguish and this pain
Moving this city to destruction.

Things are moving in the city of Hartford,
Moving slowly, barely visibly

Toward the recognition that
Only love can cast out hate and fear.

Things are moving in the city of Hartford,
In tiny movements scarcely noticed
To replace the racism at the root
Of the cancer moving through our city.

Things are moving in the city of Hartford,
But we need to move much faster
To bring healing to the city
While the heart of Hartford still beats.

(September 14, 1993)

It's not easy to love
While you experience fear.
It is not easy to look my neighbor in the eye,
If I suspect that he would do me harm.
It's not easy to love my neighbor
In the city.

It's not easy to say I'm sorry
For what I and mine have done to you and yours.
Such words may make me vulnerable, appearing weak
When I feel the need to show my strength
To keep in check the violence of my neighbor
In the city.

It's not easy to accept
That you, my neighbor, have such problems too;
That you too fear the hurts that I have given you
And which you fear I still may do again,
Adding to our mutual distrust
In the city.

It's not easy to see
How together we might overcome
This fear, this violence, this anger and this hate;
How together we might join hands
And build a better fear-free place
In the city.

It's not easy to see past
The obvious and hyped up images we see on TV
And read of in the papers;
To see past that to those who've cast out fear
And are bringing changes
To our cities.
It's not easy, but I'll try.

I'll hold my hand out to my neighbor.
I'll ask forgiveness for the wrongs
That I and mine have done.
And we'll move on to action
Till love has cast out fear
In the cities.

(June 28, 1993)

Among the most telling news stories to come out of the plight of the inner cities was the account of a ten-year-old girl who had carefully written down instructions for her own funeral. She did not expect to live many more years, given what life was like in her neighborhood. It disturbed me greatly to acknowledge the fact that an inner-city child of nine might have no greater expectation of future life than I have, living in a comfortable suburb at the age of sixty-nine.

This poem is dedicated to Sarah Smith.

To an Inner-City Child, Who, But for the Color of Her Skin, Might Be My Granddaughter

I have lived sixty-nine years.
You have lived nine.
The sad fact is that as of now
Your life expectancy is no better than mine.

One of your friends planned her funeral.
She wanted to look real nice
As her friends gathered round her coffin
To say their last "Good-bye."
Death comes with a throw of the dice.
Maybe the finger on the trigger
Belongs to a kid who is no bigger
Than you.
The bullet could kill me, but more likely you.
And really it is not funny,
We old ones have screwed up the world
And you pay the price for it, honey.

Maybe the clock shows a quarter to twelve.
Just a little time remains.
And I promise you, child, I *will* do my best
To help release you from your chains.

I know what efforts it's going to take.
I know it too well, I'm no fool,
Before you can walk safely and proud
As you go from your home to your school.
It needs all of us, honey,
To put these things right
So that you can go home at the end of the day
And sleep safely in bed through the night.

But we'll do it, if my folks can work with your folks.
We'll do it if all of us care.
We may not make it in my lifetime
But we will in yours. That's my prayer.

(Caux, August 2, 1994)

I have spent nearly a third of my life in Africa, so it is natural that much of my poetry concerns that continent. In 1985 I was a delegate to the annual roundtable of the African Association for Public Administration and Management, which was held in Accra, Ghana. The subject of the roundtable was the food crisis in Africa. At a session led by the women delegates that dealt with the role of women in food production in Africa, the male delegates were belittling the role of women in African agriculture, even though approximately 85 percent of the agricultural work in Africa is done by women. I felt strongly that something should be done to bring the debate back on track and to give proper acknowledgment to the role of African women. So on the spot I wrote the following poem, which I read out to the conference without disclosing where it came from. It was greeted with both laughter and applause, and the tone of the debate changed for the better.

It's cool beneath the shade of the tree
Where I sit and drink my beer,
But I've really earned the right to rest
For, look, the bush is clear.

I cleared the bush with muscle and sweat.
See what my labor has wrought.
So now the women can plant the seed
And work as women ought.

I cleared the ground, a vital task
Essential to producing food,
So now the women can dig with sticks
In the way that women should.

I cleared the bush, as I said before,
And made my contribution,
So now the women can tend the crops
And deal with the harvest and distribution.

I cleared the bush, as well you know,
So why should I do more?
And it's not my job to prepare the food
For cooking's a woman's chore.

I make the decisions, the important ones,
As is only natural, no doubt,
And I understand what women need,
So what are they worried about?

The women and I, we each do our part.
We both of us do our share.
And now I'm ready to eat the food.
Just give me what is fair.

But why's there so little on my plate?
Not enough to keep me fat.
Woman, give me some of yours
For I can't live on that!

(Accra, Ghana, December 5, 1985)

Nigerian Memories

Majestically the Niger and the Benue
Flow towards each other and the sea.
Overhead the circling vultures
Can see the beginnings of the desert to the north
And in the east the shallow giant lake.

Here on earth feet stamp
In joyous rhythmic dancing.
Laughter and gaiety mingle
With stately pomp and courtesy,
Ignoring for the time
The poverty of the villages.

Kind hearts and smiling faces,
Arguments, shouting, and noise;
Noise of blaring transistors.
Noise of ceaseless car horns.
Noise of people, noise of drums.

Unmindful of the noise the patient, quiet cattle
Pass on their long wanderings.
An old man kneels in the red dust of the road,
Calling out greetings to a horseman.
A large car hoots past,
Swirling red plumes of laterite at its heels.

Inside a large, richly robed rascal
Lolls back on embroidered cushions
Well pleased with life and himself.
He hears the drumming as his car
Whisks him through the village
Where the market is busy, crowded.

The small barefooted boy,
Schoolbooks in attaché case atop his head,
Hears it too and hurries home.

(First published in Nigeria Magazine,
December 1967)

Evening in Nairobi National Park

Through the tall green grass
A pair of silvery jackals pass
And on the plain
A family of cheetahs rest.
Sitting up, they look towards the west
Where kongoni and gazelle are grazing.

Close to the path
Where a dignified lone eland walks
A flock of maribou storks
Stands in committee,
Each looking like a seedy city gent
Bent on evil intent.

For the warthog passing by
They show no concern
And ignore the bristly defiant flag
Flying from his stern.

Small birds sing in the fading sun.
Zebras turn and run.
Watch how the sinking sun
Does cast
Gigantic shadows
Of the giraffes who amble past.
Impala gather underneath the trees
As the gentle evening breeze
Presages the close of day.

One of Africa's (and the world's) great educators was Dr. J. E. K. Aggrey, who worked for many years at Achimota College in Ghana. It was he who promoted women's education in Ghana on the grounds that "if you educate a man, you educate an individual, but if you educate a woman, you educate a family." The badge on the blazer proudly worn by Achimota students showed the black and white keys of a piano. Aggrey and his coworkers firmly believed that the future of the world depended on people of all colors working together. Aggrey is the "wise man" in the following poem.

A wise man in Africa said it,
And it's still very true, I own,
That you can get some sort of tune from the piano
When you use the white keys alone.
And it's equally true you can do so
By just playing the notes that are black
But unless you use both black and white keys
There's so much your music will lack.
So let's all make music together
And let the true harmony win
But it's going to take all of us, black, white, and brown
Or whatever the shade of our skin.

I can love you, my brother,
Though your skin color's different from mine.
And I can love you, my sister,
Recognizing the spark divine,
The spark divine that is in us,
Regardless of race or creed.
For we all of us hurt when we're injured
And we all spill red blood when we bleed.
We all have our hopes for the future
For ourselves and our kids, we can say.
We want freedom from fear and from hunger

And worthwhile work for fair pay.
We want to see justice for all
Though it may seem a distant dream.
But I am perfectly sure this is part
Of the Great Spirit's overall scheme.

So let us stop hurting each other
Or stop just averting our gaze.
Let's be honest about the wrongs of the past
Then move on to far better days.
We'll have to join hands together
If we're ever to get the job done
And the clock says it's quarter to midnight
But it's still not too late to have fun,
To have joy in a newfound freedom
To rejoice with newfound friends
But we'd best hurry up and build this new world
Before our old one ends.

(June 23, 1993)

Meditation on a Piece of Bread

This morning at breakfast I had a piece of bread
And in that piece of bread
I found so many things to be grateful for.
There were people.
There were those who cut the bread and put it on the
table.
There were those with whom I was having breakfast
and sharing the bread.
Then, going back, there were those who had baked the
bread,
Those who had ground the flour,
The farmers who had grown the wheat and provided
the other ingredients for the bread.
There were the farmers' wives who worked in the
home and on the farm and who enabled the farm to
be productive.
So there were so many people to be grateful for.

But then I realized that there was far more to be grateful for;
The grain from which the bread was made would
never have grown
If it were not for the sun and the rain and the earth,
which nourished the grain.
And the bread had to be cut and eaten on a plate, and I
put butter and jam on it.

So I was grateful to more than the people who had
made these things: to the earth that yielded up the iron
ore from which the knife was made, and to the cows
that gave the milk for the butter, and to the trees that
gave the fruit for the jam, and to the plants that gave the
wherewithal to make the sugar for the jam.

So many people, so many living, growing plants and animals, so many aspects of the natural world—all in that piece of bread.

And I pray for everyone to have that bread. I pray that each of us will take only what we need and see that all other beings—human, animal, and vegetable—receive what they need.

And I pray that we will cease our practices of taking more than our share and that we will cease all practices that harm the soil, the air, the rain, the sunlight, the plants, the animals, our neighbors, and ourselves.

And I thank the piece of bread I ate, which gave me energy, and everyone and everything that made it possible.

(Caux, August 10, 1994)

Every book of verse should contain love poems. Here are a few I'd like to share.

Come, my love, let us away
And we'll be gay
Both night and day,
Reveling in the joy we find
Each in the other's body and mind.
Every shade of darkness lightened,
Every joy and pleasure heightened,
Because we share
Because we dare
To love
And of our love be not ashamed.

(Perhaps I should state here that that poem was written before the original meaning of the word "gay" was replaced by its current usage.)

As light as down
That's borne upon the wind
Are thoughts of love,
As insubstantial
And as fleeting
As the presence
Of a heady favorite fragrance.

No one knew
When first you and I
Looked at each other
And saw.
No one else saw
What we could see,
Because it wasn't there
For anybody else
But you and me.

Why are you happy
To be with me?
I have no special magic
Except for you.
Why do you look at me
With such a special look?
Is that the way
I look at you
When I am happy
Just because
I'm with you?

I like it here
And I will stay.
I'll stay with you.
This "here," this "now"
Knows no geography
Or time.
This "here" is anywhere
Your presence is.
This "now"
Is when we are together.
All other times are "then"
And if you are not here
The place is "there."
Please let me live in here and now
And stay away from there and then.

She is bright, brighter than gold.
She is young, yet her smile is old,
As old as time perhaps or even older.
I get a glimpse, looking over memory's shoulder,
Of some eternal feeling, felt now,
Felt in the past, and still in future to be felt.
But where and why and how?
Such questions cannot properly be dealt with now.
No need even to guess the answer.
Let imagination, that liberated blithe romancer,
Supply all we need to know,
That having caught a dream we will not let it go.

A song of love is seldom sung
When you're climbing upwards rung by rung,
For the energy goes into the climb
And you seldom find you have the time.

But it's time to take time,
So a song I'll sing
And let my mind and body bring
Its gifts and tributes up
Until they fill a loving cup
Which I can pass to you to drink
And you can pass back to me.
We are on the very brink
Of finding something beautiful to see,
A bit from you, a bit from me,
A bit that comes from God knows where,
Sunlight and blossom and fresh air
That imparts that windswept look to your hair.

Love isn't orderly.
Love is wild,
An impetuous and unruly child
That doesn't know its place
And needs to wash its face.

A song of love is sometimes sung
When, at close of day, the bell is rung.
So keep on listening for the chime
And you will know when it's the time.

When I am a spirit
And you are alone,
Call to me
And I'll surround you.
I will bear you up
Until your storms have passed.

When I am the wind
And you are a flower,
I'll send a soft and cooling breeze
On each hot summer's day.

When I am a cloud
And you are a tree,
My gentle rain will fall on you
Till you grow strong.

When I am the thunder,
My roars and lightning
Will scare away your enemies
And all my storms
Will bring a following calm to you.

But right now I'm me
And you are you,
So I will only do
All that I can for love.

The Lovers

And then there were two
Who sat and talked,
Heads close together,
Oblivious of others,
Smiling, laughing
And obviously at ease,
As though basking
In some invisible sunlight.

I see them and recollect
Such moments as I've shared
In just this way
With some other
When all barriers
Of self-defense
Were put aside.

In such moments
Love takes root
And blossoms,
A strong and healthy growth.
Such moments are timeless
And eternal,
Never to be lost.

Poem for John and Lucia's Wedding

This business of two persons
Pooling resources,
Sharing everything they can,
Becoming responsible
Each for the other
Seems to be a pretty ingrained
Habit of the human race,
No matter what may be said
About the institution of marriage.

Not many of us
Are so truly self-possessed,
So truly independent,
That we can stand alone
Without the feeling
That we need another
To share and merge with
To be a more completed entity.

And so we start
Making tentative approaches
To others
Who might be the partners
That we seek.
Our judgment in this
Is fallible
As is our judgment
In most other things.

But at some point,
If we are fortunate,
We may feel with greater

Certainty than we have felt before,
That this is the one,
That this time we will be complete
And whole,
That we will grow
By giving,
By sharing,
By a merger
With just this one person,
Which would not be so
With all the rest.

When this is so,
Then we have reached
A turning point.
Such synergy
Can last us all our lives
And we'll be richer persons
Till we die.
Our giving brings immense returns
And not only two
But many more
Are touched by it.

This is the ideal.
But for the lucky ones
It is so very real.

Wedding Day

Today is, of course, quite different
From any other day.
It has a special quality
That's all its own
But cannot be defined.

And you, both of you,
Will be a little different now
From what you were before.
You may look a little different
So friends will notice.
You will feel different,
Still you,
But in some alchemic way
Altered.

We, your family and friends,
Rejoice with you
Because it is our sincere belief
That both of you will gain
From this step you take today.

Why do we need a ritual
To set a seal
Upon your new mutual state?
Perhaps no ritual is necessary
But a wedding is a happy thing
Where hope and love and trust
And confidence are aired.
Such things are never found in surplus
So it is right that they are shared.

(For John and Lucia)

In this silence
I gaze into your eyes
And I see love.

In this silence
I look into my heart
And I see love.

In this silence
I reach out my hand to you
To feel the touch of love.

In this silence
The truth rings in my ears
Reverberating through my being.

In this silence
I recognize
The completeness of my love.

I just want you to know
Another's heart beats faster
Because of you.
I just want you to know
My blood flows warmer in my veins
Because of you.
I just want you to know
That you are loved,
That there's another life that's richer
Just because you live,
Because you're you.
I just want you to know.

Lament of an Asian Communist Activist
on the Death of His Wife

She was all I had,
Human, living, warm and kind.
She was all I needed.
No one like her will I ever find.

> When I was weak she was my strength.
> When I was tired she was my rest.
> When courage failed she was my hope.
> In everything she was the best.

She was all I knew
Of love and warmth and tenderness.
She was always true
To all those things
That in our hearts
We both believed in.

> And it was through her care for me
> I've had the power to be free,
> Free to fight that men might live
> In freedom and equality.

But I must go on
Although my life is shattered now she's gone.
She would have it so,
And on and on
Until the better world she dreamed of
We have reached,
I'll go.

This next poem is adapted from a Vietnamese folk song.

Must you go, my lover,
Must you go?
I love you very much, you know.
Can't you stay
For just another day?
Do you really have to go away?

Must you leave, my darling,
Must you leave?
I do not find it easy to believe
You did not mean the loving words you said.
They are stored in memory in my head.
You have meant so much to me
I can't believe that it could be
That you would leave.

Must you depart, my love,
Must you depart?
And leave me here with a broken heart?
After all the times we've spent together, you and I,
I did not think the time might come to say
    "Good-bye"
Or that such love could die.

Must you stay, my dear,
Must you stay?
You told me you would go away.
And I am not a child
And so I reconciled
Myself to life without you.
I did not doubt you.

For you see, my dear,
You made it very clear
That you would go.
So now, my friend, you should know
I have found a love quite new,
But, my dear, it isn't you.
So I'll wish you "Godspeed" on your way.
And now, just go away.

(Hanoi, March 1992)

I spent happy weeks and months working as a consultant on management training in Pakistan. I know of no nation where the making of verses is enjoyed so thoroughly. So both the participants in the management training workshops and I would try to outdo each other in writing verses as the training program proceeded. The one that follows is on the subject of cost-benefit analysis.

My son, my son, it's time to marry.
You are old enough so do not tarry,
Accept your responsibilities like a man
And make the very best choice you can.

My father, my father, I heed your words,
But human beings are not like birds,
Choosing a mate just on basis of sight,
Looking for the female with plumage most bright.

My son, my son, what you say is true
And here is my advice to you.
Don't choose a wife on the basis of looks.
There are other things like how well she cooks.

Before you even start to woo
Do what evaluators do.
Cost-effectiveness you'll find is just the tool
To stop you making yourself a fool.

Figure out what the cost will be
Of marrying each of the brides to be.
How much will she spend on gems, clothes and
　　things?
How much will it exceed the dowry she brings?

They all will cost you dear, I know.
If you marry a poor girl, time will show
She may not be as demanding as one
Whose family is rich, for whom spending is fun.

The one who is going to cost you less,
According to cost-effectiveness,
Is the one you should marry, my son most dear.
Have I made my meaning clear?

My father, my father, your words are wise.
They've removed the veil from my eyes.
You have talked of costs, I note, with care.
Is there anything else I should be aware?

My son, my son, your question is just.
There is another thing that you must
Take into account when you make your choice,
Now listen to my words and hear my voice.

Marriage will bring you benefits too.
I hope this will be clear to you,
And unless the benefits exceed the cost
The advantages of marriage will be lost.

Some benefits can be quantified,
Like dowry which I've identified,
But others in cash cannot be measured,
Although they are greatly to be treasured.

My father, my father, you have helped me decide.
It is Zarin who will be my bride,
For every time I am with her
I feel a deep feeling within me stir.

The world seems to be a more beautiful place
Every time I see her face.
Her voice is sweet like a bird's song.
I know I will love her my whole life long.

The benefits cannot be measured, you're right,
Of the joys of living day and night
With this girl, the queen of all my dreams.
The choice is quite simple now it seems.

My son, my son, your analysis I take
Has been calculated without mistake.
If so, I will visit her father, Hussein,
And make the proposal to him quite plain.

And he will speak to his daughter Zarin,
Whose beauty is great and intellect keen,
So that she can work out on her calculator
If the benefits to her than the costs are greater.

My Computer Has an Attitude

My computer has an attitude—a bad one. Or perhaps that's not fair really, because it does not have it all the time. Most of the time it behaves quite nicely and politely. You could even call it user-friendly. Its underlying bad attitude shows up only when I'm writing letters or documents using WordPerfect, and even then it is only when I am using the spellchecker that its pent-up anger really comes out. It seems to have a definite bias against my female friends and relations, and I wonder if this could be based on jealousy. For example, whenever I mention my good friend Trish, the spellchecker stops on her name and malevolently suggests that I should refer to her as "trash." On the other hand, it cannot quite make up its mind about my wife's niece Sonita, for it suggests that I should call her either "sonata," which suggests someone pleasant and melodic, or "cyanide," which is deadly poison. My vibrant young cousin Vicky is quite unfairly described as "icky." Only occasionally does my computer indicate approval of women. It apparently approves of my African American friend Muriel by coming up with two alternatives, "moral" and "mayoral," though as far as I know, Muriel has no political ambitions. Does my computer know something that I don't?

To make it clear that it is not entirely sexist, it attacks my male friends too. For example, it insists that my friend Dick Ruffin should be called "ruffian" and that Hassan represents "hassle." My wife's clear-sighted nephew Vijay, an MBA student, it labels "vague" and her cousin Amerjit can be either "embargoed" or "emerged." My intensely busy and active professorial friend Dr. Harold Sandstrom it perspicaciously nicknames "sandstorm." But my French friend Jacques could never honestly be described as "gauche" or "gawkiest," as my computer insists. However, I think perhaps the worst insult concerns the late Mzee Jomo Kenyatta, the first president of Kenya. My computer balks at each part of his name and seems to think that this distinguished statesman was an overweight transvestite from a distinguished political dynasty, since it wants to call him "Ms. Jumbo Kennedy."

It even makes fun of place names. The town of Ife in Nigeria, one of the hotter parts of the world I have been to, it calls "ice." For Arusha in Tanzania, it suggests "earache," maybe because of the noise I used to make on our Hammond organ there. As for Kaduna in the north of Nigeria, where I spent many years and wrestled with many headaches, it jokingly suggests that the town should be called "codeine."

(April 7, 1994)

I would attain merit
By singing loud and clear
The beauty of creation.
Enlightenment may lie this way,
That I can see the Buddha nature
Shining through the eyes
Of every face I see.
I have far to go
Upon this pilgrimage
And I'll not yet attain
Release from the seemingly unending
Cycle of rebirth, pain, sorrow
And suffering.
And yet I grow a little closer
When I hear the Buddha nature
In the singer's song
And see it in your smile,
Hear it in your laughter.
And with this peace
Within my heart
I can sometimes
Look into the mirror,
Into my own eyes,
And see the Buddha nature
In my heart as well.

When time lies broken in the dust
And space annihilates all distance
And our spirits sink into the void
Where nothing is

When thinking's done and feeling's gone
And breath is breathed out of our bodies
And numbness holds us in a total grip
And nothing is

When pain and joy, pleasure and hurt
And love and hate are all the same
And neither good nor bad have any meaning
As nothing does

And we float on and on through endless waves
And slowly we discover once again
The core that's left and does not die
Though all else does

Then we will know us finally,
Our essence,
And with that fearful knowledge once accepted
Peace.

Be nothing.
Be empty.
Be nothing but a vessel
Into which may flow
Love,
Understanding,
Compassion,
Care for the earth
And everything
And everyone
That lives here.

Be nothing
But an opening
Through which
Goodness may enter,
God's conduit.

Be nothing
But a wire
Along which
Such a current
May flow
That can empower us
And all we touch.

This collection would not be complete without poems from Thailand, which has become my second home. The poem that follows commemorates a young classically trained Thai dancer who was part of a touring group that performs the folk theater known as likay. This folk art form combines singing, dancing, and melodrama. It is seldom seen by foreigners but is still popular in the towns and villages of Thailand, despite the inroads made by television.

A Dirge for the Dancer
Who Died Too Young

In the spirit of the dance
He brought romance and drama.
In the spirit of *likay*
He told a story.

There were love songs.
There were sword fights.
There was romance
And betrayal.
There was life
And there was death.
The dance revealed it all.
And yet we never knew
It was his own life he danced.
It was his own dance he lived.

Wherever there are people
Gathered round a stage
Watching the action
Of the men in their ancient costumes,
Of the women in their bright nylon ball gowns,
Watching the fights with wooden swords,

Enraptured by the handsome youth
With brightly painted face
Or falling for the singer
With her long eyelashes
And her heavy makeup,
All illusion,
Wherever this exists
He is there.

He is the spirit of the dance,
The spirit of *likay,*
Forging the link between
Illusion and reality;
Opening a little door
Through which folk
Can escape a while
Into a wonderland
And forget the harshness
Of their daily lives.

A short life, maybe,
And one filled with troubles
But also filled with love.
But in the spirit of the dance
He lives on,
For the spirit of the dance
Can never die.

This poem was written in Hua Hin in 1981. At that time, Hua Hin was a relatively quiet fishing village, which was a popular resort among the Thai people. There was one big old hotel there, run by the railroad company. It did not cost a lot to stay there, and for two years running (1980 and 1981) I spent about six weeks there, running courses in project management for Thai government officials, many of whom have remained my friends to this day. There was a beautiful beach, though the jellyfish were troublesome when you went swimming. Although both trainers and participants worked extremely hard and the training was very demanding, we all had a thoroughly enjoyable time there.

Alas, Hua Hin today is rather different. It has become a major tourist resort and is no longer so idyllic or cheap. I prefer to remember it as it was.

The bright early morning sun
On the white tablecloth
Is dazzling,
Too bright for eyes
Accustomed to the paler light
Of cooler climes.

There is so much here
That's dazzling,
More colorful.
No wonder that I find myself
Confused.
It isn't perfect,
Though at first it may seem
Nearly so.

The garden of Eden
May have had these very flowers,
This climate and this sandy beach,

But Adam did not work
Twelve hours a day
And Eve's brow was not
So worried, furrowed.
She never had to ponder
The problems of cost-benefit
Or microeconomics
Or stay up until the early hours
Working on her model project.
But all the same
I doubt she had as much
Laughter and friendship as we do
In this, as yet unspoilt, little town
Of Hua Hin.

Well, this has been pretty serious stuff up to now, and I think it is time for a change. Here are a few pieces of nonsense.

The donkey who sat on a thistle
Complained that he'd ruined his lunch.
His braying was spoiling my appetite
So I gave him some coleslaw to munch.
I was eating Kentucky Fried Chicken
Which Colonel Sanders had cooked
But the ass didn't think much of it.
I could tell by the way he looked.
I gave him a roll and butter
But he didn't even say "Thanks."
I was too tired anyway
And I hate to be bothered by cranks.
For donkeys are only human
And you really can't blame them much.
Their conversation is Greek to me
And their braying is double Dutch.
But, as luck would have it, my picnic
Included a bottle of beer.
I drank it myself, didn't share it,
I'd like to make that clear.
For though I'm a bit of a boozer,
And some would say I'm an ass,
I'd never serve booze to a donkey,
Especially one that's on grass.

Great Scott, your room's a frightful mess!

Darling, I love you,
That there's no gainsaying.
Your different moods
Still puzzle, startle,
Frighten me,
And so I'm glad to find
Unwavering consistency
In one respect.

Great Scott, your room's a frightful mess!

Darling, your forthrightness
Is something that will take
Some getting used to.
And the wobbling back and forth
Of Libran scales can be quite maddening.
So I find comfort in
Your one unwavering predictability.

Great Scott, your room's a frightful mess!

Darling, I find your near perfection
Hard to live up to.
How can a clumsy ectomorphic Celt compete?
So I thank God that I need feel
No way inferior
Each time I look inside your room.

Great Scott, your room's a frightful mess!

Fairy Tale
(definitely Grimmer than Hans Anderson's)

Once upon a time, in a little kingdom, there lived the young and reasonably attractive daughter of a poor charcoal burner. They lived in a little cottage in the forest. By the way, Mrs. Charcoal Burner lived there too.

Now, some years ago, the young and handsome—or at least tolerably presentable—Prince had disappeared. The rumors said that he had been changed into a dragon by a wicked witch. In the meantime, his kingdom was ruled by a Council of Wise Men, of whom the charcoal burner was one. The others were a paunchy monk fond of telling ribald stories, a knight in rather rusty armor, and the local moneylender. The charcoal burner's daughter had been brought up on tales of wicked witches, fiery dragons, and handsome princes who fell in love with poor young maidens, so she found the situation full of interesting possibilities.

One day she went walking in the forest and—yes, you've guessed it—lost her way. She wandered on and on and was beginning to get really worried. She heard a rather frightening noise, a bellowing, a crashing about, then out of a cave emerged a large green reptilian creature. Although she had never seen one before, she knew at once that this was a dragon, so she wisely hid behind a tree.

When night began to fall, she began to feel cold. As all good charcoal burners' daughters know, she could light a fire by rubbing two dry sticks of wood together. So she laid a fire and started rubbing sticks. Her hands got blistered after about half an hour but she had not produced a flame. So engrossed did she become that she failed to see the dragon watching her from behind a bush. At last, unable anymore to bear to see the wretched girl's unsuccessful attempts, he waddled over to the fire she'd laid and breathed out deeply once, setting the thing ablaze.

"Oh, my!" she cried, a little startled by the suddenness. "Thank you, dragon. Now I can keep warm, but you rather scared me." The dragon could not speak, but answered with a quiet roar.

And so they spent the night together there, and by the time the dawn arrived, the two had got quite friendly. The girl—her name was Esmeralda, by the way—was stroking the dragon and tickling his belly in a playful way.

About the middle of the day, they started hearing dogs barking and sounds of much activity throughout the forest. The charcoal burner, finding his daughter had not returned all night, had raised the alarm, and a full search was now in progress.

At last the sounds drew very close to where they were. "Oh, dear," cried Esmeralda, "I guess they've come to look for me. You'd better hide." She tickled his tummy one last time and kissed him lightly on the snout.

A blinding flash was seen. The dragon disappeared and in his place there stood a man, mid-fortyish, who still bore on his face traces of good looks. His clothes were far too tight, but after all, he'd been much younger by some twenty years when first changed to a dragon.

"Esmeralda," said the Prince, "as I'm sure you must have guessed, you have freed me from the wicked witch's spell. So according to the rules, I must ask you to be my wife and you must accept. But if you think I am too old for you, I will not take offense. As for me, I know I could do worse, and you will make a reasonably beautiful princess, so I rather hope you will say yes."

Overcome by the romantic nature of this sudden proposal and making a rather rapid mental survey of the eligible young men in her village, Esmeralda decided to accept the Prince. So when the rescue party finally reached the clearing in the forest, they found the Prince and Esmeralda in as passionate an embrace as they felt the circumstances did dictate.

The Prince went back to his rather drafty royal castle and made the charcoal burner a duke. (Mrs. Charcoal Burner really enjoyed being a duchess and being addressed as "Your Grace" by all the neighbors.) The Council of Wise Men was charged with arranging the royal nuptial ceremonies. Esmeralda looked quite fetching in her silver lamé wedding gown and, as for the Prince, he looked quite young again. Not a day, you would have thought, over thirty-eight.

That's about all really. The Council of Wise Men was made the Cabinet. The monk was made Archbishop, but was told to modify his risqué stories. The knight became Commander in Chief of the Royal Boy Scout Troop, and the moneylender followed his natural bent as Royal Tax Collector. As for the Prince and Esmeralda, both lived reasonably happily ever after. Both of them were healthy and, after all, if you've got your health and eat right and sleep right, you've got about everything.

I dueled with my friend for long.
For years the clashes of our swords
Brought sparks and noise
As steel met steel
As we each sought to penetrate
Our opponent's defenses.
Our skills have grown
And both our swords are sharper now.
I thank you, my antagonist,
My helper and my friend.

Breakfast at the Yale Club

The dark-suited ones are serious.
Their world is very small and shrinking.
They need to keep their wits about them
Helped by the coffee that they're drinking.

Their dark suits are an armor,
Cloaks of invisibility
Since they all look alike
In uniformed anonymity.

The office men, that's what they are,
With hardly a woman to be seen
For women might break up the pattern
And disturb the safe familiar scene.

Theirs is a world of serious meetings,
Business lunches, files and faxes.
Theirs is a world of power struggles.
It's not a world where one relaxes.

I feel for the dark-suited men
For whom life is earnest every hour
And taken as a whole it's true
They wield a deal of power.

But I do wish they would relax,
Give up their uniforms, and smile,
And see the whole of life
And not just what's in the file.

And if they did I wonder what
The dark-suit brigade could do.

The satisfaction they could get
From their work would be quite new.

Suppose they changed the way
They went about their tasks.
They could stop covering their backs.
They could take off their masks.

Perhaps they could really learn to serve,
Work for the common good,
Not worrying about their own position.
Do you think they really could?

I know an office man or two
Who's managed to do just that.
They walk to work with a spring in their step
And they always have time to chat.

They seem to have an inner strength
That comes from deep inside.
And they're not only men, they're women too.
They work with humble pride.

They seem to have a purpose
That goes beyond getting through the day
They're less worried about their status
And don't let it get in the way.

They listen to an inner voice
And believe in doing what's right,
Which may sound pompous and heavy
But you find their touch is light

And somehow they seem to get results
That surprise us. We wonder how.

For they're very down-to-earth people
And they live in the here and now.

But they all seem to have a faith
In some power that's greater than they,
And they all seem to live by a moral law
Which they believe is the Way.

And they're cheerful folk to be with.
They seem to enjoy their lives.
I wish the dark suits could all be like that
And I bet so do their wives.

(New York, September 16, 1994)

The Last Word

Good-bye, my friend.
This is the end.
I've enjoyed our little walk
And the interesting talk.

We seem to agree
That, as far as we can see,
The state of the world is sad.
It really is too bad.

Pollution, greed, and crime
Are in the news all the time.
Street violence increases
And drug peddling never ceases.

Society's decay
Seems to get worse every day,
But what are we do,
I mean folks like me and you.

But I guess the truth, my friend,
Is quite simple in the end
And we've really always known it,
Though we've often failed to own it.

It's not difficult to see
That change must begin with me,
For there is no other soul
Over which I have control.

And if everybody saw
That there's a universal law

Which will always clearly state
That hate can never put an end to hate.

But forgiveness and goodwill,
Sometimes a bitter pill
To swallow, can create
The climate to end violence and hate.

If we take just what we need,
Forgoing all our greed,
There will be enough to share,
So that all can get what's fair.

And this goes for not just
The material things we lust
For, but for other things that bait us
Like sex, wealth, power and status.

And you'll find that more and more
We see that at the core
Of all the great faiths of the world
The same truths have been unfurled.

So listen to the inner voice
Which every day makes clear the choice
You have, to be part of the cure.
Of this you can be sure.

We can turn back the tide.
It starts from deep inside.
The power of love is on our side
And it will never be denied.